Matty and Moe are two happy frogs.

They like to play on rocks and make rafts from tiny logs.

One day Matty bragged to Moe, "I'm a very tall frog. I bet I can hop longer hops than you."

"But Matty," croaked Moe, "I'm a very big frog, and I hop long hops too."

"Let's find out," said Matty. "I bet I can get to the big rock in fewer hops than you, because my hops are longer."

"But my hops are bigger," said Moe. "I'll go first and show you."

He stretched his large legs and started hopping.

It took him 5 hops to get to the big rock.

Moe croaked, "Now see if you can beat that. READY, STEADY, HOP!"

It took Matty 2 hops more than it took
Moe to get to the big rock.

How many hops did it take Matty to get
to the rock?

It took Moe 5 hops.

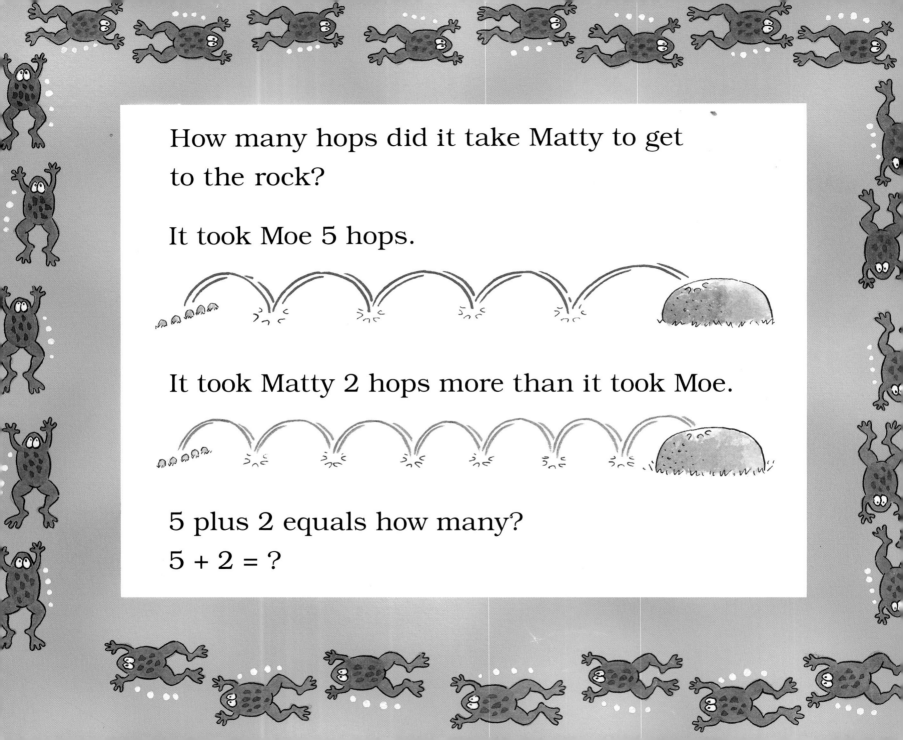

It took Matty 2 hops more than it took Moe.

5 plus 2 equals how many?
5 + 2 = ?

"I can't believe it," said Matty. "You took fewer hops, so you're ahead so far. But now let's hop to the hollow log."

Moe wasn't worried. He knew he could
hop longer hops.

It took him 7 hops to get to the log.

"Okay, Matty, it's your turn—
READY, STEADY, HOP!"

Matty hopped 3 hops fewer than Moe to get to the log.

How many hops did it take Matty to get
from the rock to the log?

It took Moe 7 hops.

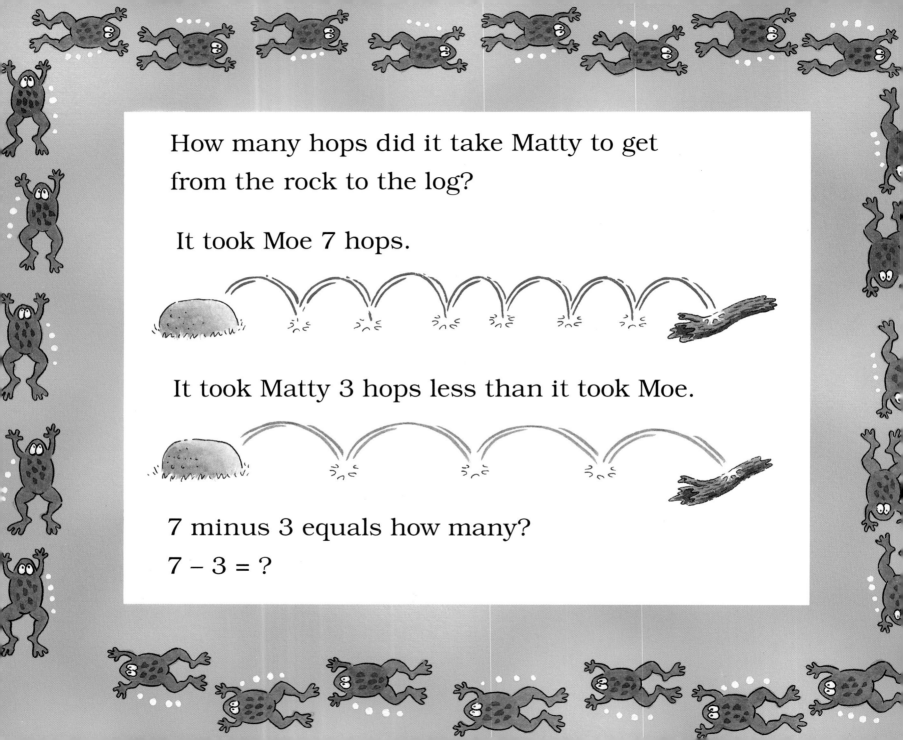

It took Matty 3 hops less than it took Moe.

7 minus 3 equals how many?

7 – 3 = ?

Matty said, "We were each ahead one
time, so we'd better try once more."
"Okay," said Moe. "Watch how few hops
I take to get to the pond."

"After you, Moe," said Matty.

With 7 long hops, Moe reached the pond.

"Come on, Matty," yelled Moe. "READY, STEADY, HOP!"

Matty hopped and hopped. He hopped 2 hops more than Moe—but he should have stopped and hopped 1 less.

How many hops did Matty take to get from the log to the pond? How many should he have taken?

It took Moe 7 hops.

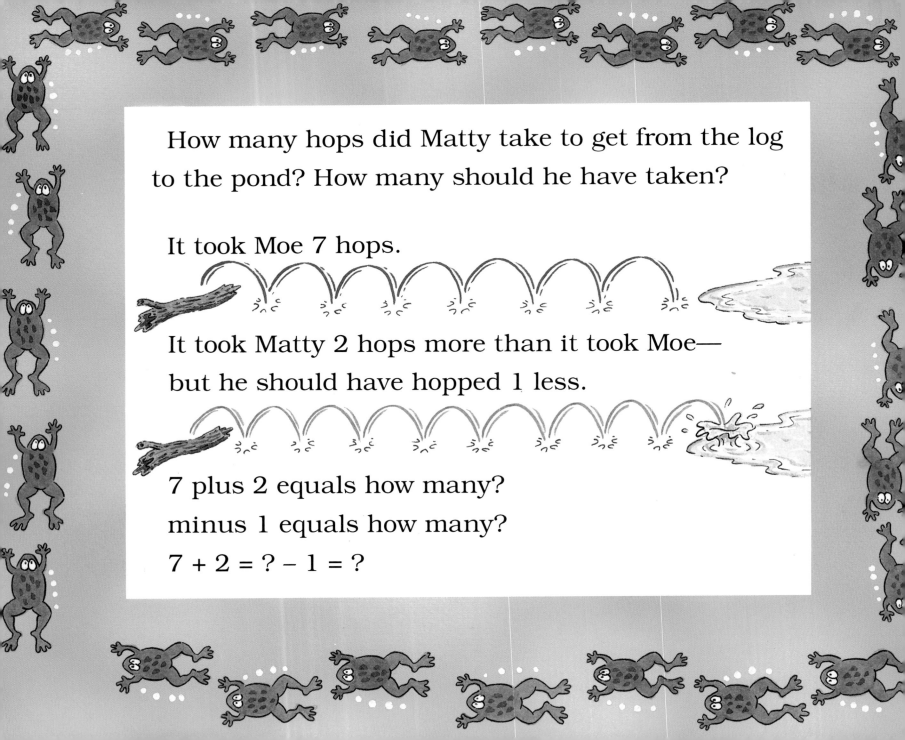

It took Matty 2 hops more than it took Moe— but he should have hopped 1 less.

7 plus 2 equals how many?

minus 1 equals how many?

$7 + 2 = ? - 1 = ?$

Moe croaked, "The contest is over. Let's add up all our hops and see who won."

Moe counted: "I hopped 5 hops to get to the rock, then 7 more to the log—and 7 more to the pond. That gives me 19 hops."

Matty said, "I hopped 7 and 4 and 9. That makes 20 hops in all. It looks like you finished with one hop less than me. So Moe, you're the better hopper."

"I won! But all that hopping made me hot," croaked Moe. "Watch out! I'm hopping in."

Matty said, "If you take one more hop,

19 + 1 = 20

then both of us will win!"

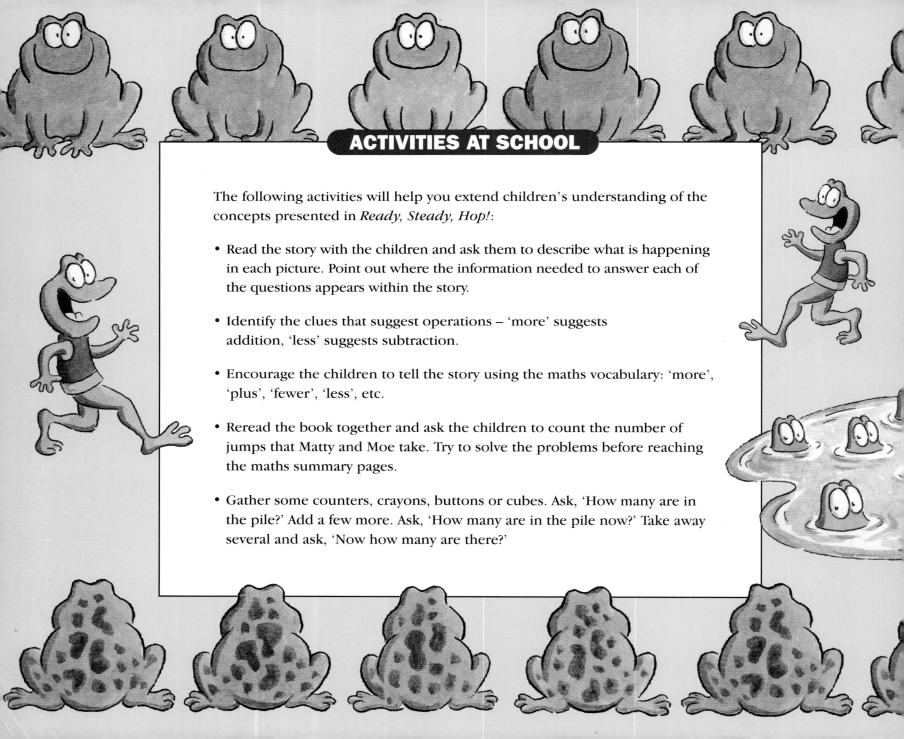

ACTIVITIES AT SCHOOL

The following activities will help you extend children's understanding of the concepts presented in *Ready, Steady, Hop!*:

- Read the story with the children and ask them to describe what is happening in each picture. Point out where the information needed to answer each of the questions appears within the story.

- Identify the clues that suggest operations – 'more' suggests addition, 'less' suggests subtraction.

- Encourage the children to tell the story using the maths vocabulary: 'more', 'plus', 'fewer', 'less', etc.

- Reread the book together and ask the children to count the number of jumps that Matty and Moe take. Try to solve the problems before reaching the maths summary pages.

- Gather some counters, crayons, buttons or cubes. Ask, 'How many are in the pile?' Add a few more. Ask, 'How many are in the pile now?' Take away several and ask, 'Now how many are there?'

ACTIVITIES AT HOME

If you would like to have fun with the maths concepts presented in
Ready, Steady, Hop!, here are a few suggestions:

- After reading the story with your child, ask him or her to retell it in
  his or her own words.

- Look at things in the real world and work together to create addition and
  subtraction problems. Examples could include pets: two dogs plus one
  cat equals three pets; or fruit: five apples minus two apples equals
  three apples.

- Place a few biscuits on a plate and, as more biscuits are added and
  some are eaten, ask, 'How many biscuits are on the plate now?'

- Draw a family tree. Determine how many people are in your
  immediate family. Add grandparents, aunts, uncles or cousins.
  Now ask, 'How many people are in your family? How many
  children are in your family?'

- Pick a book. Tumble it end to end to measure the number of
  book lengths from one room to two other rooms. Which
  distance is less? Which is more? How many more or less?